T0070653

Benedetto
MARCELLO

(1686 – 1739)

Sonata for Flute and Basso continuo, Op. 2 No. 7
B-flat Major / Si bémol majeur / B-Dur

Edited by
Mechthild Winter and Thomas Reimann

DOWANI International

Preface

Thomas Reimann, freelance flautist and lecturer at the Hochschule für Musik und Theater Leipzig, has performed this Sonata for Flute and Basso Continuo op. 2 No. 7 in B-flat Major by Benedetto Marcello, and has arranged the flute part. The sonata first appeared in print in 1712 in Venice, in a collection of twelve sonatas. It was later also published in Amsterdam and London, which is testimony to the international renown already enjoyed by the composer during his lifetime. Our edition allows you to study this piece systematically and in three varying tempi with professional accompaniments.

The CD opens with the concert version of each movement (flute and basso continuo). After tuning your instrument (Track 1), the musical work can begin. Your first practice session should be at slow tempo. If your stereo system is equipped with a balance control, you can place either the flute or the harpsichord accompaniment in the foreground by adjusting the control. The flute always remains softly audible in the background as a guide. In the middle position, both instruments can be heard at the same volume. If you do not have a balance control, you can listen to the solo part on one loudspeaker and the harpsichord part on the other. After having practised this piece at a slow tempo, you can proceed to practise the second, fourth and fifth movements at a moderate tempo. We have decided against offering moderate tempo versions of the first and third movements, since the originals of both are relatively slow. Now you can play the piece with accompaniment at the original tempo. At the medium and original tempos, the continuo accompaniment can be heard on both channels (without flute) in stereo quality. All of the versions were recorded live. The names of the musicians are listed on the last page of this volume; further information can be found in the Internet at www.dowani.com.

The articulation markings in the solo part are original; editorial slurs, ornamentation, and variations in dynamics have deliberately been omitted to allow the musician freedom to try out several possibilities and in so doing to learn to deal with these stylistic means of interpretation. In keeping with the standard modern transcription of B-flat Major, a flat sign (♭) has been added to the key signature, but the accidentals in the basso continuo have been left in the original.

The realisation of the basso continuo offered here is limited to one possible basic realisation of the figured bass with a few ideas on rhythm and dynamics (reduction of number of parts to two or three parts). It was not possible to print out the many various possibilities offered by the harpsichord, such as a full accompaniment, ornamentation, or arpeggio accompaniment, since they are largely dependent on the technical skill and taste of the accompanist, and also have to suit the soloist's interpretation. Accompanists who are familiar with playing basso continuo will be able to play from the figured bass part.

We wish you lots of fun playing from our *DOWANI 3 Tempi Play Along* editions and hope that your musicality and diligence will enable you to play the concert version as soon as possible. Our goal is to provide the essential conditions you need for effective practicing through motivation, enjoyment and fun.

Your DOWANI Team

Avant-propos

Thomas Reimann, flûtiste en free-lance et professeur à l'École Supérieure de Musique et Théâtre de Leipzig, a enregistré la présente Sonate pour flûte et basse continue op. 2 No. 7 en Si bémol majeur de Benedetto Marcello et a réglé la partie de flûte. La sonate parut en 1712 à Venise dans uns collection de 12 sonates. D'autres éditions à Amsterdam et Londres suivirent. Cela démontre la réputation internationale dont jouissait le compositeur déjà de son vivant. Notre édition vous propose d'étudier l'œuvre de manière systématique dans trois tempos différents et avec un accompagnement professionnel.

Le CD vous permettra d'entendre d'abord la version de concert de chaque mouvement (flûte et basse continue). Après avoir accordé votre instrument (plage n° 1), vous pourrez commencer le travail musical. Votre premier contact avec le morceau devrait se faire à un tempo lent. Si votre chaîne hi-fi dispose d'un réglage de balance, vous pouvez l'utiliser pour mettre au premier plan soit la flûte, soit l'accompagnement de clavecin. La flûte restera cependant toujours très doucement à l'arrière-plan comme point de repère. En équilibrant la balance, vous entendrez les deux instruments à volume égal. Si vous ne disposez pas de réglage de balance, vous entendrez l'instrument soliste sur un des haut-parleurs et le clavecin sur l'autre. Après avoir étudié le morceau au tempo lent, vous pouvez étudier les deuxième, quatrième et cinquième mouvements également au tempo moyen. Concernant les premier et troisième mouvements, nous avons renoncé au tempo moyen, puisque leurs tempos originaux sont déjà relativement lents. Vous pourrez ensuite jouer le tempo original. Dans ces deux tempos vous entendrez l'accompagnement de la basse continue sur les deux canaux en stéréo (sans la partie de flûte). Toutes les versions ont été enregistrées en direct. Vous trouverez les noms des artistes qui ont participé aux enregistrements sur la dernière page de cette édition ; pour obtenir plus de renseignements, veuillez consulter notre site Internet : www.dowani.com.

Les phrasés dans la partie du soliste sont d'origine. Les éditeurs se sont sciemment abstenus de rajouter des liaisons, ornements et indications pour la dynamique afin de laisser à l'interprète toutes les possibilités d'exploration et de se familiariser avec ces moyens stylistiques. L'indication de la tonalité Si bémol majeur à la clé a été adaptée afin de se conformer aux usages actuels. En revanche, les altérations dans le chiffrement de la basse continue sont originales.

Notre édition se borne à une réalisation basique de la basse continue, comportant quelques suggestions concernant le rythme et la dynamique (réduction du nombre des voix à deux ou trois). Les nombreuses possibilités de réalisation, comme le jeu à pleine main, les ornements ou encore les arpèges, ne peuvent pas être présentées dans ce cadre puisqu'elles dépendent essentiellement du savoir-faire et du goût de l'accompagnateur et doivent aussi être en corrélation avec l'interprétation du soliste. Les accompagnateurs familiers avec la basse continue peuvent directement utiliser la partie de basse chiffrée.

Nous vous souhaitons beaucoup de plaisir à faire de la musique avec la collection *DOWANI 3 Tempi Play Along* et nous espérons que votre musicalité et votre application vous amèneront aussi rapidement que possible à la version de concert. Notre but est de vous offrir les bases nécessaires pour un travail efficace par la motivation et le plaisir.

Les Éditions DOWANI

Vorwort

Thomas Reimann, freischaffender Flötist und Dozent an der Hochschule für Musik und Theater Leipzig, hat die vorliegende Sonate für Flöte und Basso continuo op. 2 Nr. 7 in B-Dur von Benedetto Marcello eingespielt und die Flötenstimme eingerichtet. Die Sonate ist 1712 in einer Sammlung von 12 Sonaten erstmals in Venedig im Druck erschienen, später auch in Amsterdam und London. Dies spricht für die international anerkannte Stellung des Komponisten bereits zu seinen Lebzeiten. Unsere Ausgabe ermöglicht es Ihnen, das Werk systematisch und in drei verschiedenen Tempi mit professioneller Begleitung zu erarbeiten.

Auf der CD können Sie zuerst die Konzertversion (Flöte und Basso continuo) eines jeden Satzes anhören. Nach dem Stimmen Ihres Instrumentes (Track 1) kann die musikalische Arbeit beginnen. Ihr erster Übe-Kontakt mit dem Stück sollte im langsamen Tempo stattfinden. Wenn Ihre Stereoanlage über einen Balance-Regler verfügt, können Sie durch Drehen des Reglers entweder die Flöte oder die Cembalobegleitung stufenlos in den Vordergrund blenden. Die Flöte bleibt jedoch immer – wenn auch sehr leise – hörbar. In der Mittelposition erklingen beide Instrumente gleich laut. Falls Sie keinen Balance-Regler haben, hören Sie das Soloinstrument auf dem einen Lautsprecher, das Cembalo auf dem anderen. Nachdem Sie das Stück im langsamen Tempo einstudiert haben, können Sie den zweiten, vierten und fünften Satz auch im mittleren Tempo üben. Beim ersten und dritten Satz haben wir auf das mittlere Tempo verzichtet, da sie im Original schon relativ langsam sind. Anschließend können Sie sich im Originaltempo begleiten lassen. Die Basso-continuo-Begleitung erklingt im mittleren und originalen Tempo auf beiden Kanälen (ohne Flöte) in Stereo-Qualität. Alle eingespielten Versionen wurden live aufgenommen. Die Namen der Künstler finden Sie auf der letzten Seite dieser Ausgabe; ausführlichere Informationen können Sie im Internet unter www.dowani.com nachlesen.

Die Artikulationsbezeichnungen in der Solostimme sind original; auf das Hinzufügen von Bindungen, Verzierungen und dynamischen Differenzierungen ist bewusst verzichtet worden, um dem Spieler oder der Spielerin das Ausprobieren verschiedener Möglichkeiten offenzulassen und so den Umgang mit diesen stilistischen Gestaltungsmitteln zu erlernen. In der Vorzeichnung wurde nach der heute üblichen B-Dur-Schreibweise ein ♭ ergänzt, die Akzidentien in der Generalbass-Bezifferung wurden aber original beibehalten.

Die Aussetzung des Generalbasses beschränkt sich auf eine mögliche grundlegende Realisierung des bezifferten Basses mit einigen Ideen zu Rhythmus und Dynamik (Reduzierung der Stimmenanzahl auf drei oder zwei Stimmen). Die vielfältigen Gestaltungsmöglichkeiten am Cembalo wie vollstimmiges Spiel, Verzierungen oder Arpeggiogestaltung sind in diesem Rahmen nicht darstellbar, denn sie obliegen dem Können und musikalischen Geschmack des Begleiters und müssen mit der Interpretation des Solisten korrespondieren. Begleiter, die mit dem Generalbassspiel vertraut sind, können aus der bezifferten Bassstimme spielen.

Wir wünschen Ihnen viel Spaß beim Musizieren mit unseren *DOWANI 3 Tempi Play Along*-Ausgaben und hoffen, dass Ihre Musikalität und Ihr Fleiß Sie möglichst bald bis zur Konzertversion führen werden. Unser Ziel ist es, Ihnen durch Motivation, Freude und Spaß die notwendigen Voraussetzungen für effektives Üben zu schaffen.

Ihr DOWANI Team

Sonata

for Flute and Basso continuo, Op. 2 No. 7
B flat Major / Si bémol majeur / B-Dur

B. Marcello (1686 – 1739)
Continuo Realization: M. Winter

© 2007 DOWANI International, 6332 Hagendorn, Switzerland

DOW 5516

5

*Autograph: Measures 6–19 are repeated ‖: :‖

6

Flute

Sonata

for Flute and Basso continuo, Op. 2 No. 7
B flat Major / Si bémol majeur / B-Dur

I ②

B. Marcello (1686 – 1739)
Edited by T. Reimann

*Autograph: Measures 6–19 are repeated 𝄆 𝄇

© 2007 DOWANI International, 6332 Hagendorn, Switzerland

DOW 5516

II **3**

Allegro

III ④

Largo

Gavotta ⑤

Allegro

Minuet ⑥

*Gavotta da Capo ***

Sonata

for Flute and Basso continuo, Op. 2 No. 7
B flat Major / Si bémol majeur / B-Dur

I

B. Marcello (1686 – 1739)

*Autograph: Measures 6–19 are repeated ‖: :‖

© 2007 DOWANI International, 6332 Hagendorn, Switzerland

DOW 5516

II

Allegro

III

Largo

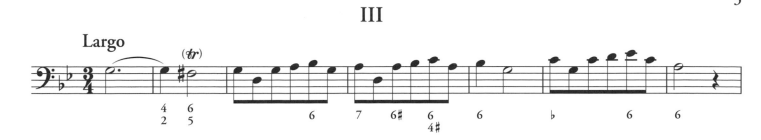

Gavotta

Allegro

Minuet

Gavotta da Capo

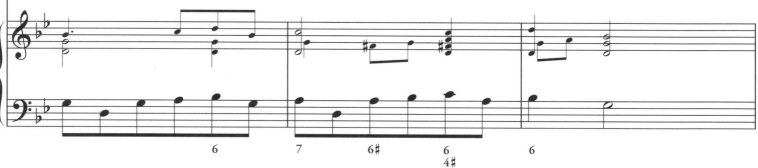

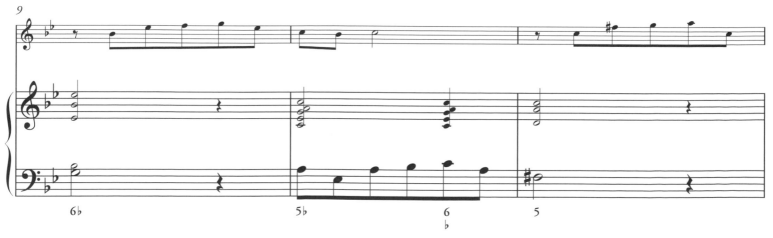

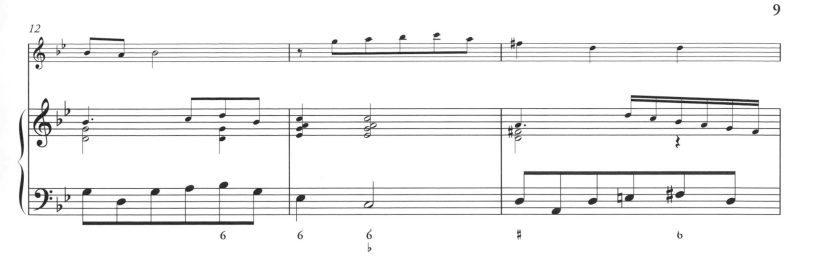

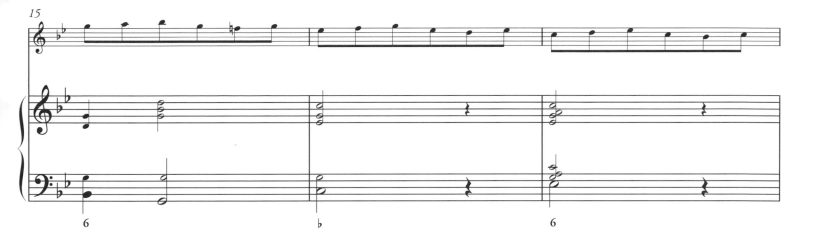

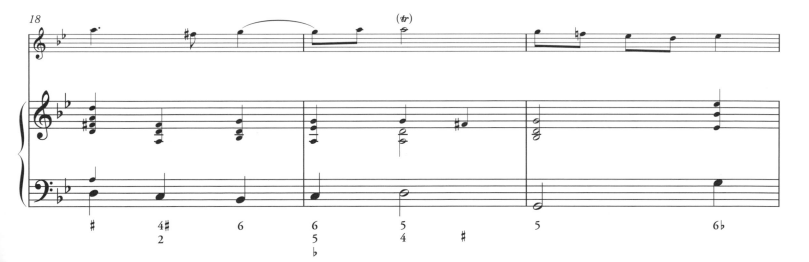

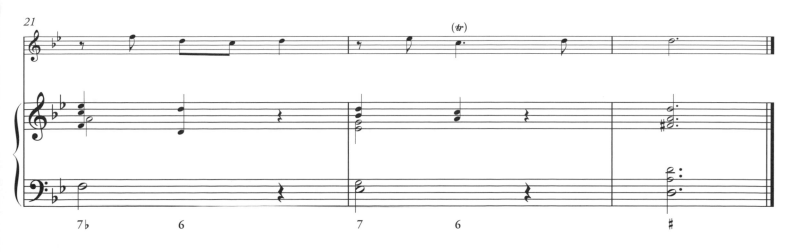

Gavotta

Minuet

Gavotta da Capo

Gavotta da Capo

ENGLISH

DOWANI CD:
- Track No. 1
- Track numbers in circles
- Track numbers in squares

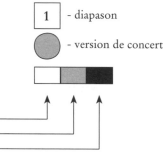

- slow Play Along Tempo
- intermediate Play Along Tempo
- original Play Along Tempo

- **1** - tuning notes
- - concert version

- Additional tracks for longer movements or pieces
- **Concert version:** flute and basso continuo
- **Slow tempo:** channel 1: flute solo; channel 2: harpsichord accompaniment; middle position: both channels at the same volume
- **Intermediate tempo:** basso continuo only
- **Original tempo:** basso continuo only

Please note that the recorded version of the harpsichord accompaniment may differ slightly from the sheet music. This is due to the spontaneous character of live music making and the artistic freedom of the musicians. The original sheet music for the solo part is, of course, not affected.

FRANÇAIS

DOWANI CD :
- Plage N° 1
- N° de plage dans un cercle
- N° de plage dans un rectangle

- tempo lent play along
- tempo moyen play along
- tempo original play along

- **1** - diapason
- - version de concert

- Plages supplémentaires pour mouvements ou morceaux longs
- **Version de concert :** flûte et basse continue
- **Tempo lent :** 1ᵉʳ canal : flûte solo ; 2ⁿᵈ canal : accompagnement de clavecin ; au milieu : les deux canaux au même volume
- **Tempo moyen :** seulement l'accompagnement de la basse continue
- **Tempo original :** seulement l'accompagnement de la basse continue

L'enregistrement de l'accompagnement de clavecin peut présenter quelques différences mineures par rapport au texte de la partition. Ceci est du à la liberté artistique des musiciens et résulte d'un jeu spontané et vivant, mais n'affecte, bien entendu, d'aucune manière la partie soliste.

DEUTSCH

DOWANI CD:
- Track Nr. 1
- Trackangabe im Kreis
- Trackangabe im Rechteck

- langsames Play Along Tempo
- mittleres Play Along Tempo
- originales Play Along Tempo

- **1** - Stimmtöne
- - Konzertversion

- Zusätzliche Tracks bei längeren Sätzen oder Stücken
- **Konzertversion:** Flöte und Basso continuo
- **Langsames Tempo:** 1. Kanal: Flöte solo; 2. Kanal: Cembalobegleitung; Mitte: beide Kanäle in gleicher Lautstärke
- **Mittleres Tempo:** nur Basso continuo
- **Originaltempo:** nur Basso continuo

Die Cembalobegleitung auf der CD-Aufnahme kann gegenüber dem Notentext kleine Abweichungen aufweisen. Dies geht in der Regel auf die künstlerische Freiheit der Musiker und auf spontanes, lebendiges Musizieren zurück. Die Solostimme bleibt davon selbstverständlich unangetastet.

DOWANI - 3 Tempi Play Along is published by:
DOWANI International
A division of De Haske (International) AG
Postfach 60, CH-6332 Hagendorn
Switzerland
Phone: +41-(0)41-785 82 50 / Fax: +41-(0)41-785 82 58
Email: info@dowani.com
www.dowani.com

Recording & Digital Mastering: Wachtmann Musikproduktion, Germany
Music Notation: Notensatz Thomas Metzinger, Germany
Design: Andreas Haselwanter, Austria
Printed by: Zrinski d.d., Croatia
Made in Switzerland

Concert Version
Thomas Reimann, Flute
Mechthild Winter, Harpsichord
Isolde Winter, Baroque Cello

3 Tempi Accompaniment
Slow:
Mechthild Winter, Harpsichord

Intermediate:
Mechthild Winter, Harpsichord
Isolde Winter, Baroque Cello

Original:
Mechthild Winter, Harpsichord
Isolde Winter, Baroque Cello

© DOWANI International. All rights reserved. No part of this publication may be reproduced, stored, in a retrieval system, or transmitted in any form or by any means, electronic, mechanical, photocopying, recording, or otherwise, without the prior permission of the publisher.